My Baby's

1st Year

My baby's
Love

Published in 2019
by Igloo Books Ltd
Cottage Farm
Sywell
NN6 0BJ
www.igloobooks.com

Copyright © 2019 Igloo Books Ltd
Igloo Books is an imprint of Bonnier Books UK

0819 001.01
2 4 6 8 10 9 7 5 3 1
ISBN 978-1-78905-708-9

Designed by Dave Chapman
Edited by Claire Ormsby-Potter

Printed and manufactured in China

Contents

— Before You Were Born —

The day we found out you were coming

Photo
MEMORIES

We are your parents

Hi, I'm your _____

_____

_____

_____

_____

Hi, I'm your _____

_____

_____

_____

_____

Small
BUMP
Photos

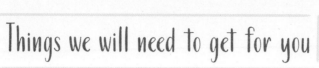

Things we will need to get for you

1. _____
2. _____
3. _____
4. _____
5. _____
6. _____
7. _____
8. _____
9. _____
10. _____
11. _____
12. _____
13. _____
14. _____
15. _____
16. _____
17. _____
18. _____
19. _____
20. _____

Getting ready for you to arrive

Your
SECOND
Scan

Big
BUMP
Photos

BIGGER
Bump Photos

Name ideas

Important People You Need To Meet

Waiting For You To Arrive

I hope that you

I hope you love

I hope you never forget

I hope you grow

_____

_____

_____

I hope you become

_____

_____

_____

I hope

_____

_____

_____

What we called you before you were born

_____

— You've Been Born—

You were born... ☐ on time ☐ early ☐ late

It took _____ for you to arrive

Your eyes were _____

Your hair was _____

Your First
PHOTO

How we spent our first day together

Look How Small You Were!

Hand print

Foot print

Date

You weighed as much as

You were as long as

— Coming Home —

You came home on...

This was the photo we sent to tell
people you were here!

This is your nursery

This is your home

— Your Fabulous Firsts —

First visitors

First bath

First time you sat up

First time you rolled over

First time you crawled

First time you stood up

First time you walked

First time you smiled

First time you laughed

Your first word

Your first solid food

First time you clapped

Your first tooth

Your first haircut

First time you slept in your own room

First time you slept through the night

First time staying with someone else

First day out

First holiday

1 Month

Photo
MEMORIES

This month you learned how to...

We did lots of...

— You're Growing! —

You are now as big as...

2 Months

Things that make you happy...

Photo
— MEMORIES —

This month you learned how to...

We did lots of...

— You're Growing! —

You are now as big as...

3 Months

Photo
MEMORIES

Things that make you happy...

This month you learned how to...

50

We did lots of...

— You're Growing! —

This is how much you grew!

4 Months

Photo
MEMORIES

Things that make you happy...

This month you learned how to...

We did lots of...

— You're Growing! —

You are now as big as...

5 Months

Things that make you happy...

This month you learned how to...

_____

_____

_____

_____

We did lots of...

— You're Growing! —

This is how much you grew!

6 Months

Photo
MEMORIES

Things that make you happy...

This month you learned how to...

We did lots of...

— You're Growing! —

You are now as big as...

Photo
MEMORIES

Things that make you happy...

This month you learned how to...

We did lots of...

_____

_____

_____

_____

_____

— You're Growing! —

This is how much you grew!

8 Months

Things that make you happy...

photo
— MEMORIES —

This month you learned how to...

We did lots of...

— You're Growing! —

You are now as big as...

9 Months

photo
MEMORIES

Things that make you happy...

This month you learned how to...

We did lots of...

— You're Growing! —

This is how much you grew!

10 Months

Photo
MEMORIES

Things that make you happy...

_____

_____

_____

_____

_____

This month you learned how to...

_____

_____

_____

_____

We did lots of...

_____

_____

_____

_____

— You're Growing! —

You are now as big as...

11 Months

Things that make you happy...

Photo
— MEMORIES —

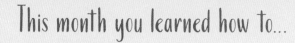

This month you learned how to...

We did lots of...

— You're Growing! —

You are now as big as...

12 Months

Photo
MEMORIES

Things that make you happy...

_____

_____

_____

_____

_____

This month you learned how to...

We did lots of...

— You're Growing! —

 This is how much you grew!

— Your First Birthday! —

These were your presents!

This is how you spent your day

Special Occasions

When was this?

Who was there?

You most enjoyed...

— Special Occasions —

When was this?

Who was there?

You most enjoyed...

— Our Trips —

Where?

When?

We went with...

The best part was...

— Our Trips —

Where?

When?

We went with...

The best part was...

Our Best
Pictures
From This Year

Photo
MEMORIES